THIS BOOK BELONGS TO:

(your name)

_____

and

(hamster's name)

_____

❦   In memory of:
Mary, Chispa, Peggy, Mrs Frisby, Floppy, Keko,
Boleta, Walter, Rosie, Mooi and Roko. Thanks
for all the happiness you brought into our lives.

❦   Credits:
Illustrations by Marie is Great
Graphic Design by Treewood Designs
info@treewood.es
Edit Tools Icon by Smalllikeart www.flaticon.com
Other Icons by Freepik www.flaticon.com
Pea Missy and Max Fonts by fontsforpeas.com

The information printed herein represents the view of the author as of the date of publication. The author reserves the right to alter and update his/her opinions. While every attempt has been made to verify the information in this book, the author does not assume any responsibility for errors, inaccuracies or omissions. The information in this book is not a replacement for veterinary advice.

First Edition

Copyright © 2020 Animal Lake Books

ISBN: 9798649156158

HAMSTER MASTER

CARE GUIDE & ACTIVITY BOOK FOR CHILDREN

Written by Jenny Laguna

ANIMAL LAKE BOOKS

AMSTERDAM BARCELONA
TOKYO SÃO PAULO

CONTENTS

CARE AND FUN ACTIVITIES

Names are important!

🌰 My hamster's name:

🌰 Why I picked this name:

🌰 What other names did I consider?

Draw or place your
hamster's picture here

My hamster's description

🌰 **Type/Breed:**
- ○ Syrian Hamster
- ○ Dwarf Hamster (see the opposite page)

🌰 **Sex:**
- ○ Male
- ○ Female

🌰 **Approximate Age:**

🌰 **Color:**

🌰 **Fur Type:**
- ○ Short
- ○ Long

Dwarf hamster breeds

There are a variety of dwarf hamsters. They can be quite hard to tell apart.

If you own a dwarf hamster and know its breed, please indicate which it is:

○ Campbell's

○ Winter White

○ Roborovski

○ Chinese

○ Other

Please note: Campbell's, Winter White and Roborovski are also frequently grouped as "Russian hamsters."

Did you know...

Hamsters are nocturnal animals, that is, they sleep most of the day. They are active at night, so please be respectful of their sleeping needs!

Let's get the hamster a nice home!

What you need:

1. An escape proof hamster cage.

2. A hamster house or nesting box.

3. Bedding, ideally aspen, pine or recycled-paper. Don't use cedar wood shavings as it can be toxic.

Draw or place your
hamster's house picture here

4. An exercise wheel.

5. A hamster water bottle.

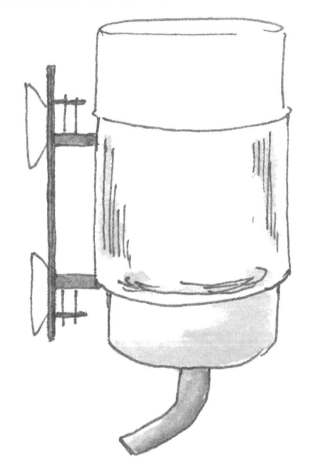

6. Hamster food-mix.

7. Optional: a hamster exercise ball and treats.

Settling in

Ideally you should only get your hamster once you have the cage set up.

Stress can make the hamster sick. The trip, new smells, new noises... it's quite a lot for a little one!

Put the cage in a dry, quiet, draft-free spot, safe from other pets.

Cover the cage with a cloth for a few days so it can get used to the environment.

Feeding

Your hamster needs to be fed and given fresh water **at least twice a week.**

Here's what he/she needs:

1. Clean water.

2. A bowl of hamster food-mix.

3. A small piece of fruit or vegetable. Please use the table on the opposite page as guidance.

4. An occasional treat. ☺

Once a week pamper your hamster with a few store-bought hamster treats, a nut, 3-5 unsalted sunflower seeds, or a dandelion flower or two! (Other flowers can be poisonous.)

Did you know...

Hamsters can run up to 5 miles (9 km) a day!

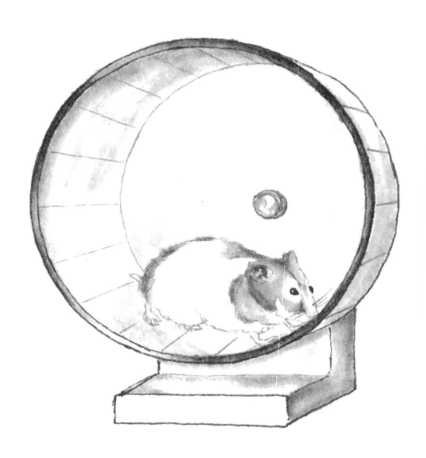

Which words best describe your hamster?

Please circle those that apply:

HAPPY

FLUFFY

FRIENDLY

HYPER

SMART

SLEEPY

HUNGRY

FUN

TINY

GRUMPY

NOISY

ATHLETIC

CUTE

MESSY

Fruits and vegetables

Not all fruits and vegetables are good for hamsters. Some can give them a stomachache or even be poisonous!

APPROVED	FORBIDDEN
Broccoli	Onions
Parsley	Garlic
Apple	Tomatoes
Pear	Lettuce
Carrot	Potatoes
Strawberry	Oranges

Just a small piece of fruit is enough. Hamsters can actually develop a disease called diabetes from eating too much sugar from fruit.

My hamster's favorite treats

Favorite:

2nd favorite:

3rd favorite:

What's your favorite treat?

Did you know...

Hamsters are solitary, that is, they like to live alone and will only tolerate each other for mating!

Getting Your Hamster Used to You

1st Make sure your hammie is happy and healthy. Remember, he/she needs quality food, fresh water and a spacious clean cage with a running wheel.

2nd Resist!!! It's reaaallly hard but please wait at least 2 or 3 days before trying to pick him/her up. Remember, hamsters can nip!

3rd Spend time speaking to your hamster softly, so he/she gets used to your voice and scent.

4th Pamper your hamster with special treats! Sunflower seeds are a favorite, kind of like ice-cream for us, so don't give him/her too much.

Do you have any tips?

Five fun things to do

1. **Imitate** a hamster eating.

2. **Pretend** you are a hamster running on its wheel.

3. **Find** a dandelion to feed your hamster.

4. **Pretend** you are a hamster and fill your cheeks with food.

5. **Build** your hamster a tunnel with a couple of toilet paper rolls.

Turning your hamster into your best friend

🌰 Put a few sunflower seeds on your palm and let it walk on it and eat calmly.

🌰 Repeat daily and be very patient.

🌰 Once your hammie is comfortable eating on your palm, you can try and hold it.

It takes time to build a friendship!

How to properly hold a hamster

Hamsters can easily fall and get injured!

The best way to handle a hamster is to "cup" it softly with both of your hands then gently open your hands so that the hamster is sitting across both palms.

For safety reasons, always do this on your lap or on a table.

Tip: never grab a sleeping hamster! Chances are that he/she will nip and hurt you.

Did you know...

Hamsters are
colorblind, that is,
they can't see color.

Two truths and a lie

Which is the lie?

a) Hamsters like to eat dandelions

b) Hamsters lay eggs

c) Hamsters don't like to live in groups

Correct answer:
b) Hamsters lay eggs.

What does a hamster have in common with a bear?

Which is the correct answer?

a)They are both reptiles

b)They can both climb trees

c)They can both hibernate

Hibernation is when animals sleep for long periods of time during cold weather. This can last weeks or even months!

They do this to survive Winter by spending minimal energy. They wake up in Spring, when food is available again.

Animals that can hibernate

Some hibernating animals include hamsters, hedgehogs, bears, turtles, bats, bees and snakes.

How long do hamsters and other animals live?

AVERAGE NUMBER OF YEARS	TYPE OF ANIMAL
1	Mouse
2-3	Hamster
5	Pigeon
10	Chicken
13	Dog
16	Cat
25	Horse
70	Elephant
72	Human
100	Galapagos Tortoise
200	Greenland Shark

Extra exercise around the house!

A safe and fun way to have your hamster get a little extra exercise is to use an exercise ball.

Only use it under close supervision!

Beware of dogs, cats and young siblings. You don't want the dog or cat to scare it or your younger sibling to lose your hammie! ☹

Important:

Use the exercise ball for a maximum of 15 minutes as the hamster could get tired. He/she might also be ready to get home for some rest, sleep or a little snack!

Let's get it clean!

Once per week follow these 10 steps:

1. Wash your hands.

2. Put the hammie in a safe place, for example in an exercise ball, or in an empty bucket. Keep away from other pets!

3. Throw out ALL the old bedding and food, including what your pet has hamstered away, as it can mold (yuck).

4. Wash the cage and wheel with a mixture of warm water and cleaning vinegar.

5. Dry the cage with kitchen paper.

Let's get it clean!

6. Wash and dry the food dish.

7. Clean and refill the water bottle.

8. Add clean bedding.

9. Put the hamster back in the cage.

10. Wash your hands again and you are done!

Clean Cage
=
Happy Hamster

Did you know...

Hamsters are compulsive food hoarders!

Hamsters have pouches in their cheeks. They use them to carry food into their homes.

Draw a picture of your
hamster with full cheeks here

Help the hamster get to the sunflower seeds

Help the hamster get to the sunflower seeds (ADVANCED LEVEL!!!)

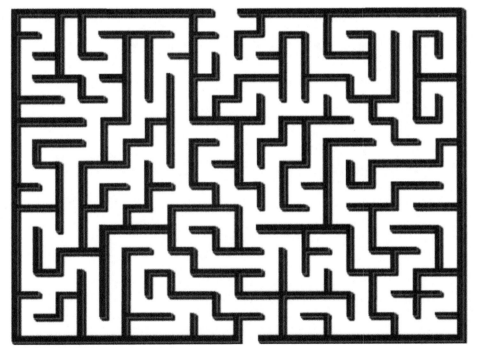

Roses are red,

Violets are blue,

I love my hammie

and he loves me too!

A letter to my hamster...

My Dear Hamster,

Love,

Did you know...

Hamsters usually give birth to 8 to 12 pups at a time.

The babies are born blind and hairless and will nurse for about 3 weeks.

Approximate weight and size

BREED	SIZE	WEIGHT
SYRIAN	15 cm / 6.5"	160 g / 5.5 oz
CAMPBELL'S AND WINTER WHITE DWARF	7.5 cm / 3"	50 g / 1.8 oz
ROBOROVSKI DWARF (THE SMALLEST BREED!)	5 cm / 2"	25 g / 0.9 oz
EUROPEAN (THE LARGEST BREED!)	28 cm / 11"	300 g / 10.6 oz

Your height in hamsters!

You might need a little help with this one!

Syrian Hamster Size: 15 cm (6.5 inches)

Your Height:

Calculation: your height divided by the hamster size

Result:

YOU ARE (result) SYRIAN HAMSTERS HEIGH!

Your weight in hamsters!

You might need a little help with this one!

Syrian Hamster Weight: 160 g cm (5.5 oz)

Your Weight:

Calculation: your height divided by the hamster weight

Result:

YOU WEIGH (result) SYRIAN HAMSTERS!

Did you know...

Hamsters don't need a bath. They wash themselves with their own spit! Cats and flies also clean themselves with their own saliva (spit).

A little bit of science and Latin

〇 Hamsters are mammals, actually rodents. They are closely related to rats and mice.

〇 They belong to the rodent subfamily Cricetidae. That's hard to pronounce - it's Latin!

〇 The scientific names for the main breeds are:

  〇 **Mesocricetus auratus**

  (Syrian)

  〇 **Phodopus campbelli**

  (Campbell's Dwarf)

  〇 **Phodopus sungorus**

  (Winter White Dwarf)

  〇 **Phodopus roborovskii**

  (Roborovski Dwarf)

Phodopus campbelli
and
Mesocricetus auratus

Other animals that begin with the letter H

1)

2)

3)

4)

5)

Some options are:
Hedgehog, hippopotamus, hare, hawk, horse, hyena, hummingbird, humpback whale, heron and hermit crab.

It's a joke!

KNOCK KNOCK

Who's there?

HAMSTER.

Hamster who?

I'M STILL WAITING FOR YOU TO OPEN THE DOOR!

It's a joke!

What runs, eats, poops and sleeps a lot?

You?

No silly! My hamster!

It's a joke!

What's a hamster's favorite city to live in?

Hamsterdam

MONTHLY CARE LOG

Instructions

 HAMSTER CARE LOG

MONTH:

WEEK	DUTY	TIMES PER WEEK	M	T	W	Th	F	Sa	Su
1	Hamster food-mix	3							
	Water	2							
	Vegetables or Fruit	2							
	Clean the cage	1							
2	Hamster food-mix	3							
	Water	2							
	Vegetables or Fruit	2							
	Clean the cage	1							
3	Hamster food-mix	3							
	Water	2							
	Vegetables or Fruit	2							
	Clean the cage	1							
4	Hamster food-mix	3							
	Water	2							
	Vegetables or Fruit	2							
	Clean the cage	1							
5	Hamster food-mix	3							
	Water	2							
	Vegetables or Fruit	2							
	Clean the cage	1							

Caring for your hamster is easy and fun!

Here's how to complete a Hamster Care Log:

1. Write in the current month.

2. Follow the weekly tasks indications. Check pages 18 for more details as necessary.

3. Mark the sheet as you complete each task. For example, feed the hamster at least 3 times a week.

4. Monthly substitute the sheet for a new one.

HAMSTER CARE LOG

MONTH:

WEEK	DUTY	TIMES PER WEEK	M	T	W	Th	F	Sa	Su
1	Hamster food-mix	3							
	Water	2							
	Vegetables or Fruit	2							
	Clean the cage	1							
2	Hamster food-mix	3							
	Water	2							
	Vegetables or Fruit	2							
	Clean the cage	1							
3	Hamster food-mix	3							
	Water	2							
	Vegetables or Fruit	2							
	Clean the cage	1							
4	Hamster food-mix	3							
	Water	2							
	Vegetables or Fruit	2							
	Clean the cage	1							
5	Hamster food-mix	3							
	Water	2							
	Vegetables or Fruit	2							
	Clean the cage	1							

HAMSTER CARE LOG

MONTH:

WEEK	DUTY	TIMES PER WEEK	M	T	W	Th	F	Sa	Su
1	Hamster food-mix	3							
	Water	2							
	Vegetables or Fruit	2							
	Clean the cage	1							
2	Hamster food-mix	3							
	Water	2							
	Vegetables or Fruit	2							
	Clean the cage	1							
3	Hamster food-mix	3							
	Water	2							
	Vegetables or Fruit	2							
	Clean the cage	1							
4	Hamster food-mix	3							
	Water	2							
	Vegetables or Fruit	2							
	Clean the cage	1							
5	Hamster food-mix	3							
	Water	2							
	Vegetables or Fruit	2							
	Clean the cage	1							

HAMSTER CARE LOG

MONTH:

WEEK	DUTY	TIMES PER WEEK	M	T	W	Th	F	Sa	Su
1	Hamster food-mix	3							
	Water	2							
	Vegetables or Fruit	2							
	Clean the cage	1							
2	Hamster food-mix	3							
	Water	2							
	Vegetables or Fruit	2							
	Clean the cage	1							
3	Hamster food-mix	3							
	Water	2							
	Vegetables or Fruit	2							
	Clean the cage	1							
4	Hamster food-mix	3							
	Water	2							
	Vegetables or Fruit	2							
	Clean the cage	1							
5	Hamster food-mix	3							
	Water	2							
	Vegetables or Fruit	2							
	Clean the cage	1							

HAMSTER CARE LOG

MONTH: _____

WEEK	DUTY	TIMES PER WEEK	M	T	W	Th	F	Sa	Su
1	Hamster food-mix	3							
	Water	2							
	Vegetables or Fruit	2							
	Clean the cage	1							
2	Hamster food-mix	3							
	Water	2							
	Vegetables or Fruit	2							
	Clean the cage	1							
3	Hamster food-mix	3							
	Water	2							
	Vegetables or Fruit	2							
	Clean the cage	1							
4	Hamster food-mix	3							
	Water	2							
	Vegetables or Fruit	2							
	Clean the cage	1							
5	Hamster food-mix	3							
	Water	2							
	Vegetables or Fruit	2							
	Clean the cage	1							

HAMSTER CARE LOG

MONTH:

WEEK	DUTY	TIMES PER WEEK	M	T	W	Th	F	Sa	Su
1	Hamster food-mix	3							
	Water	2							
	Vegetables or Fruit	2							
	Clean the cage	1							
2	Hamster food-mix	3							
	Water	2							
	Vegetables or Fruit	2							
	Clean the cage	1							
3	Hamster food-mix	3							
	Water	2							
	Vegetables or Fruit	2							
	Clean the cage	1							
4	Hamster food-mix	3							
	Water	2							
	Vegetables or Fruit	2							
	Clean the cage	1							
5	Hamster food-mix	3							
	Water	2							
	Vegetables or Fruit	2							
	Clean the cage	1							

HAMSTER CARE LOG

MONTH:

WEEK	DUTY	TIMES PER WEEK	M	T	W	Th	F	Sa	Su
1	Hamster food-mix	3							
	Water	2							
	Vegetables or Fruit	2							
	Clean the cage	1							
2	Hamster food-mix	3							
	Water	2							
	Vegetables or Fruit	2							
	Clean the cage	1							
3	Hamster food-mix	3							
	Water	2							
	Vegetables or Fruit	2							
	Clean the cage	1							
4	Hamster food-mix	3							
	Water	2							
	Vegetables or Fruit	2							
	Clean the cage	1							
5	Hamster food-mix	3							
	Water	2							
	Vegetables or Fruit	2							
	Clean the cage	1							

HAMSTER CARE LOG

MONTH:

WEEK	DUTY	TIMES PER WEEK	M	T	W	Th	F	Sa	Su
1	Hamster food-mix	3							
	Water	2							
	Vegetables or Fruit	2							
	Clean the cage	1							
2	Hamster food-mix	3							
	Water	2							
	Vegetables or Fruit	2							
	Clean the cage	1							
3	Hamster food-mix	3							
	Water	2							
	Vegetables or Fruit	2							
	Clean the cage	1							
4	Hamster food-mix	3							
	Water	2							
	Vegetables or Fruit	2							
	Clean the cage	1							
5	Hamster food-mix	3							
	Water	2							
	Vegetables or Fruit	2							
	Clean the cage	1							

HAMSTER CARE LOG

MONTH: _____

WEEK	DUTY	TIMES PER WEEK	M	T	W	Th	F	Sa	Su
1	Hamster food-mix	3							
1	Water	2							
1	Vegetables or Fruit	2							
1	Clean the cage	1							
2	Hamster food-mix	3							
2	Water	2							
2	Vegetables or Fruit	2							
2	Clean the cage	1							
3	Hamster food-mix	3							
3	Water	2							
3	Vegetables or Fruit	2							
3	Clean the cage	1							
4	Hamster food-mix	3							
4	Water	2							
4	Vegetables or Fruit	2							
4	Clean the cage	1							
5	Hamster food-mix	3							
5	Water	2							
5	Vegetables or Fruit	2							
5	Clean the cage	1							

HAMSTER CARE LOG

MONTH:

WEEK	DUTY	TIMES PER WEEK	M	T	W	Th	F	Sa	Su
1	Hamster food-mix	3							
	Water	2							
	Vegetables or Fruit	2							
	Clean the cage	1							
2	Hamster food-mix	3							
	Water	2							
	Vegetables or Fruit	2							
	Clean the cage	1							
3	Hamster food-mix	3							
	Water	2							
	Vegetables or Fruit	2							
	Clean the cage	1							
4	Hamster food-mix	3							
	Water	2							
	Vegetables or Fruit	2							
	Clean the cage	1							
5	Hamster food-mix	3							
	Water	2							
	Vegetables or Fruit	2							
	Clean the cage	1							

HAMSTER CARE LOG

MONTH:

WEEK	DUTY	TIMES PER WEEK	M	T	W	Th	F	Sa	Su
1	Hamster food-mix	3							
	Water	2							
	Vegetables or Fruit	2							
	Clean the cage	1							
2	Hamster food-mix	3							
	Water	2							
	Vegetables or Fruit	2							
	Clean the cage	1							
3	Hamster food-mix	3							
	Water	2							
	Vegetables or Fruit	2							
	Clean the cage	1							
4	Hamster food-mix	3							
	Water	2							
	Vegetables or Fruit	2							
	Clean the cage	1							
5	Hamster food-mix	3							
	Water	2							
	Vegetables or Fruit	2							
	Clean the cage	1							

HAMSTER CARE LOG

MONTH:

WEEK	DUTY	TIMES PER WEEK	M	T	W	Th	F	Sa	Su
1	Hamster food-mix	3							
	Water	2							
	Vegetables or Fruit	2							
	Clean the cage	1							
2	Hamster food-mix	3							
	Water	2							
	Vegetables or Fruit	2							
	Clean the cage	1							
3	Hamster food-mix	3							
	Water	2							
	Vegetables or Fruit	2							
	Clean the cage	1							
4	Hamster food-mix	3							
	Water	2							
	Vegetables or Fruit	2							
	Clean the cage	1							
5	Hamster food-mix	3							
	Water	2							
	Vegetables or Fruit	2							
	Clean the cage	1							

HAMSTER CARE LOG

MONTH:

WEEK	DUTY	TIMES PER WEEK	M	T	W	Th	F	Sa	Su
1	Hamster food-mix	3							
	Water	2							
	Vegetables or Fruit	2							
	Clean the cage	1							
2	Hamster food-mix	3							
	Water	2							
	Vegetables or Fruit	2							
	Clean the cage	1							
3	Hamster food-mix	3							
	Water	2							
	Vegetables or Fruit	2							
	Clean the cage	1							
4	Hamster food-mix	3							
	Water	2							
	Vegetables or Fruit	2							
	Clean the cage	1							
5	Hamster food-mix	3							
	Water	2							
	Vegetables or Fruit	2							
	Clean the cage	1							

FREE DRAWING
AND NOTES

✗ ✗✗ ✗✗ | | |

| | | | | | | |

| | |

8065 055540

saturday 2 02 nd January 2022

my day is horibie i feel like giveing up on like people dont know how it feels i feel scarde and anxious noone likes me if feel sad

bad day

HAMSTER MASTER CERTIFICATE

(your name) has successfully completed the Hamster Master training. His/her hamster must be very proud!

Signed: JENNIFER LAGUNA

Date:

ABOUT THE AUTHOR

Jenny Laguna is an animal lover who is dedicated to helping and saving animals, big or small. Daughter of a veterinarian, her first sister was a dog named Chispa. She lives in Amsterdam with her three cats and two dwarf hamsters named Kung and Fu.

ANIMAL LAKE BOOKS

AMSTERDAM BARCELONA
TOKYO SÃO PAULO

AN ENGAGED (LITTLE) OWNER MEANS A HAPPY, HEALTHY PET!

animal_lake

Printed in Great Britain
by Amazon